Wiltshire Reformatory for Boys Warminster

1856-1924

Ivor Slocombe

First published in the United Kingdom in 2005 by
The Hobnob Press, PO Box 1838, East Knoyle, Salisbury SP3 6FA

British Library Cataloguing in Publication Data
A catalogue record for this book is available from the British Library.

ISBN 0-946418-45-4

Typeset in 11/13.5 pt Scala
Typesetting and origination by John Chandler
Printed in Great Britain by Salisbury Printing Company Ltd, Salisbury

Foreword

My early interest in Victorian schools in Wiltshire led naturally on to the study of other aspects of Victorian education. With the gradual movement towards compulsory school attendance, the School Boards were important in ensuring there were sufficient schools and for setting and enforcing regulations about attendance. Where School Boards did not exist, the School Attendance Committees under the Poor Law Guardians performed a similar function. Persistent non-attendance was dealt with by fines on the parents and, in the more extreme cases, by sending children away to Industrial Schools. There was inevitably a problem over finding school places for juveniles with a criminal record and it was for many of these that the new Reformatories provided an answer.

It was therefore exciting to find that not only did Wiltshire have one of the new Reformatories but that it became recognised as one of the leading institutions in the country. The main records of the Reformatory, preserved in the Wiltshire and Swindon Record Office, had been little studied and the building itself, although converted into houses and apartments, remains substantially as it was when the Reformatory closed in 1924.

This booklet aims to chronicle the life and history of a little known institution which had great significance both for Wiltshire and, more immediately, for the town of Warminster. The study also, more generally, throws light on an aspect of Victorian penal reform and on the methods used to deal positively with juvenile offenders which may still have some relevance today.

I am most grateful to all those who have given me help and encouragement in the production of this booklet, in particular:

the staff of the Wiltshire and Swindon Record Office and of the Local Studies Library who have indicated sources which I might otherwise have missed;

my wife for her professional advice on the Tascroft building and for producing plans showing the use of the rooms;

the Tascroft residents, especially Mrs. Pam Lewis and Mrs. Pearl Williams, who generously showed me around the present building and shared their knowledge of it with me.

Introduction

The mid 19th century witnessed an interest in penal reform both of prisons and the criminal law. A particular aspect was juvenile crime and the attempt to reform young offenders through the use of reformatories rather than prison. A leading light in this movement was Mary Carpenter whose book *Reformatory Schools for the children of the perishing and dangerous classes and for juvenile offenders* was published in 1851.

There was great concern about the rapid increase in juvenile crime. In Westminster, for example, the number of juveniles convicted rose from 1098 in 1837 to 1260 in 1847. A House of Lords Select Committee also noted that the number of criminals under 20 committed to prison had increased from 6,803 in 1835 to 11,348 in 1844. This represented 1 in 304 of the total population aged 10 to 20.

The traditional attitude towards young offenders was punishment as retribution in itself but also to act as a deterrent. Thus the most common sentence was whipping (except for girls) with up to 10 strokes of the birch. Prison sentences were short, not usually exceeding a month or two and often for only a week, and were intended as a short, sharp shock rather than as a longer term confinement. But this was clearly not working as a large number of young people re-offended. 66% of male juveniles committed to prison had previous convictions and, of these, nearly 30% had been in prison four times or more. The proportion was higher for juveniles than for adults.

Mary Carpenter also argued that education as it then existed made little impact. Most of the convicted juveniles had at least some rudimentary education such as being able to write their own name and to recite the Lord's Prayer. But she concluded that 'the mere mechanical power of reading and writing, unaccompanied by sound moral, industrial and religious training, really prepares the ill-disposed for greater audacity in crime.'

The protagonists for penal reform were partly acting out of self-interest. The overwhelming proportion of juvenile crimes involved petty theft at a time when the more affluent classes saw the ownership of property, goods and chattels as all important. The increase in crime and in the number of families living on the proceeds of crime (the 'dangerous classes') represented a real threat to the foundations of their society. But there was also an altruistic, religious element in the movement. For all the reformers, moral and religious education was an essential feature of any programme. This arose partly from the Christian doctrine of love for all men and partly from the belief that the instillation of Christian principles into young people would ensure that they would become useful members of society.

Mary Carpenter's other dominating theory was that much of the juvenile offending was caused by a bad home background, whether a family in extreme poverty or one already heavily into crime, with a consequent lack of spiritual and moral guidance. Her conclusion was, therefore, that the young criminals should be taken away from this bad family influence and placed in a new type of reformatory.

These new institutions would aim 'to train up children who will be fitted to gain an honest livelihood, being a benefit to society rather than its bane'. Love must be the ruling sentiment of all who attempt to guide these children and the school should infuse a moral tone based entirely on a sense of duty to God. Discipline, order and obedience must be maintained by firmness but it was also important to engage the interest of children, with emphasis being placed on industrial training, for this was considered to develop the faculties and to have a direct moral influence. Finally attention needed to be paid to personal cleanliness, promoting the physical as well as the moral health of the scholars.

Early Reformatories

In putting forward her proposals, Mary Carpenter gave examples of existing institutions which had some elements of her suggested regime. She particularly highlighted Mettrai in France which provided for 400 boys arranged in a collection of 40 'families'. It aimed to create an atmosphere not of fear but of 'love, guided by wisdom and the experience of a sound mind'. Corporal punishment was totally prohibited but sanctions included admonitions and deprivation of meals and recreation. Some basic education in reading and writing was undertaken but the main emphasis was on industrial training.

An early example in England was at Warwick where an institution had been established by the local magistrates in 1831. Not only was this cheaper than prison, but of the 77 boys admitted, 41 were said to have been reformed. This compared with a sample of 14 juveniles committed to prison of whom 10 were subsequently re-convicted and transported. This was followed by a number of similar Reformatories across the country, all started by voluntary bodies in which the church played a leading role.

The Reformatory movement was successful in getting the establishment of a Select Committee in 1853 followed by the Youthful Offenders Act of 1854. This made Reformatory Schools established by individuals and charitable bodies subject to examination by prison inspectors. If certified as satisfactory, they could take convicted young offenders under 16 for a period of two to five years. Such offenders still had first to serve a short prison sentence. The Reformatories would be eligible for government grants but the parents were also required to make a contribution. Between August and December 1854 seven Reformatory Schools were established including Kingswood and Red Lodge, Bristol. By 1857 another 40 schools had been certified and together they had 1866 inmates (1609 boys and 257 girls).

A further Act of 1857 was aimed at encouraging more Reformatories to be established. It allowed county and borough authorities to make grants to build new schools and to extend existing ones. Most of the new Reformatories were in adapted existing buildings such as large farmhouses but 14 were in purpose-built premises. Almost all had some agricultural land, typically 10 to 30 acres.

Establishment of the Wiltshire Reformatory.

The movement to establish a Reformatory in Wiltshire was initiated and sustained by the Rev. Arthur Fane. He was the son of Sir Harry Fane, sometime C.-in-C. of the British Forces in India, and was quite wealthy eventually inheriting Boyton House from a relative. He held the living of Warminster for 18 years from 1841 to 1859 and was connected with a number of charitable activities and institutions in the town. Although the new Reformatories were opposed by some people, including the Wiltshire magistrates according to one report, he managed to enlist a powerful committee under the chairmanship of Mr. Watson Taylor of Erlestoke Park. Later the committee was enlarged to include most of the 'great and the good' in Wiltshire such as Captain Gladstone, Earl Bruce, the Earl of Suffolk, Lord Heytesbury, John Phipps and all the local M.P.s. The Reformatory maintained a very close connection with the Church and throughout its existence the Secretary or Manager was always a local vicar.

The first meeting was held at Chippenham in September 1855 and a sub-committee was charged with the task of finding a suitable site. The main requirements were that it should be within reach of as many magistrates and other gentlemen whether clerical or laity as could be obtained to take an interest in its supervision and management. They needed up to 20 acres with or without buildings and, if leased, for not less than 21 years. The site had to be within two miles of a railway station and, finally, it had to be within easy reach of a church. An advertisement in the county papers produced only one response which did not meet the requirements. They also looked at sites at Boyton and Norton Bavant but again these were felt to be too far from a station.

The solution came through an offer from Mr. Stephen White. He held 22 acres of land called Tascroft at Bugley from Lord Bath on a lease of two lives. This was two miles from Warminster station, was dry and airy yet considered very productive land with water obtainable at a depth of 50 feet. The annual rent was 48s. per acre. The only problem was that the lease, which was on the lives of two persons aged 59 and 66, did not seem to give sufficient security. Lord Bath was approached about extending the lease when it expired. He was sympathetic, explaining that he disliked the complications of leases on lives but his hands were tied and he could not take any action which would bind his successors. Eventually he agreed to the inclusion of a third life. This led to some interesting discussions about who should be nominated with suggestions which included looking for a young healthy female or perhaps William Awdry, the 14 year old son of Sir J. Awdry. The land had no buildings on it and, although this would mean incurring higher costs, it did give the committee an opportunity to have a purpose-built Reformatory and they accepted an offer from Mr. Wyatt to be their honorary architect. This was probably Thomas Henry Wyatt, a member of a nationally known family of architects who came from the Devizes area and who was best known in Wiltshire for his church architecture. Wyatt may have become involved because he was the Salisbury Diocesan architect and therefore he would have been known to Rev. Fane.

The Reformatory opened in December 1856 and local magistrates were encouraged to send to it appropriate cases of boys under the age of 14. The institution seems to have got off to a good start. In July 1858 Rev. Fane reported that there were 22 inmates and he considered the Reformatory to be doing well; 'The institution appears fully to answer the most sanguine expectations of its patrons and is deserving of more general support which it much needs.' Rev. Warburton, reporting in 1859 in his *Survey of Wiltshire Schools*, recorded that 'all 28 inmates are fed, lodged and clothed out of the funds. 22 acres of land are leased at a yearly rent of £54 4s. The officers are a master (with his wife) and an assistant labour master. The salary of the former is £91 a year and the latter receives 9s. a week.

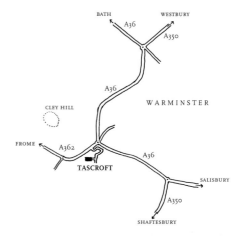

The location of the site in the modern road system west of Warminster

None are admitted but those who have been convicted by the magistrates except a very few specially recommended. Field work is intended to occupy two-thirds of the boys' time and intellectual instruction, reading, writing, arithmetic and catechism, one third. Mr. Ruddock reports that the institution, especially in writing, is satisfactory and that the influence of the master is good. Much is due, he observes, to the exertions of the vicar.' He added that he had personally visited the school and was much struck with the good manners of the boys and the cleverness of the master.

The reality, however, was less optimistic. The Reformatory was very much under the control of Rev. Fane and, although he might have been visionary in achieving its establishment, he does not seem to have been the best of managers especially in dealing with its finances. Things seem to have started to go wrong in 1860 and came to a head three years later. In February 1860 H.M. Inspectors investigated certain alleged but unspecified irregularities in the discipline and management of the Reformatory and in June the *Warminster Miscellany* reported there were rumours that dissatisfaction was still rife amongst the inmates. Then in March 1861 one of the boys, William Coster, set fire to two straw ricks and a workshop with a dormitory above. Luckily the fire did not spread to the main building.

The crisis came to a head in 1863 when Rev. Fane inherited a family living in Lincolnshire. The committee under the chairmanship of Lord Heytesbury had difficulty in getting hold of the records and of discovering exactly how the Reformatory stood financially. Eventually they calculated that there were liabilities of £540, not including the rent, while the total assets including farm stock were valued at £590. Things got worse when it became necessary to sack the master, Mr. White, who had been found drunk in the high road. The committee, after some lengthy discussion, decided they should try to continue the Reformatory rather than close it. They considered an appeal to the Quarter Sessions for financial support but most of the members preferred the institution to remain voluntary and rely on government grants and local contributions. An appeal was then made to the laity and clergy of the county in order to liquidate the outstanding debt and enable the school to start again free of 'pecuniary incumbrance'. The Rev. Bob Hutton was appointed secretary and manager at a salary of £35 a year.

The post of master was advertised both nationally and locally. Of the 58 applications received 20 were from London. A sub-committee was despatched to London to interview eleven of these at Hatchetts Hotel. Three local candidates, Mr. T. Turner, Mr. J. Low and Mr. H. Hussey the schoolmaster at Heytesbury, were also considered. The committee decided to appoint Mr. Hendley, a colour sergeant in the Scots Guards. This was controversial for Rev. Turner, the Inspector of Reformatories, had already sent a letter to one of the members of the committee opposing the appointment of any ex-military candidate: 'I hope the Committee will hesitate about the appointment of any person as Master of a Reformatory who has been a Drill or Pay Sergeant in the Army. Experience shows the qualifications for the two offices to be very different and any such selections that have hitherto been made have ended very unsatisfactorily. You could hardly make a more unsatisfactory choice except you took the warder of a prison. I write to clear myself from any responsibility (in case such a person being chosen) as to the results on the operations of the school, absconding, etc.' The committee then made further inquiries about Mr. Hendley but were reassured by personal recommendations to Lord Bath from Capt. Adj. Trefussis and Col. Charteris. They were also persuaded by the qualifications of Mr. Hendley's wife to be matron. Their joint salary was to be £50 a year with rations (for three), coals, candles and vegetables.

It was from this new start in 1863 that the Reformatory developed so successfully and earned such a high reputation over the next 60 years.

The Buildings

The Reformatory buildings at Tascroft remain virtually intact although now converted into a series of apartments. They are situated at Folly Lane, Bugley, two miles to the west of Warminster down a long lane leading off the roundabout where the A362 Warminster to Frome road crosses the Warminster by-pass. The east range incorporates the original part of the Reformatory designed by Wyatt. However, his plan was not entirely adopted. The tenders based on his design ranged from £998 to £1052 15s. but, as these were considered to be more than the committee could afford, Mr. William Hardick, a Warminster architect, was asked to revise the specifications to include the block plan of only one half Wyatt's plan with a prolongation of the building for the boys by ten feet. Three new tenders were received: Browne and Son, Frome £810, Trap £811 and Barnden £797. The tender of John Barnden, a Warminster architect and builder, was accepted in April 1856 and the building was ready to open by December. The building was of brick and flint and is one of the few domestic-style buildings known to have been designed by Wyatt.

During the 60 years of its existence the Reformatory underwent a number of alterations and extensions. In 1864 reference is made to a 'Crimean' hut used mainly as a dormitory but this was giving trouble with rain leaking through the roof. In 1869 plans were approved for a new (Crimean) wooden hut. This was to be sited near the existing dormitories and would provide an enlargement to the boys' dormitory and a sitting room and bedroom for the schoolmaster. This increased the capacity of the school from 50 to 60. Staff

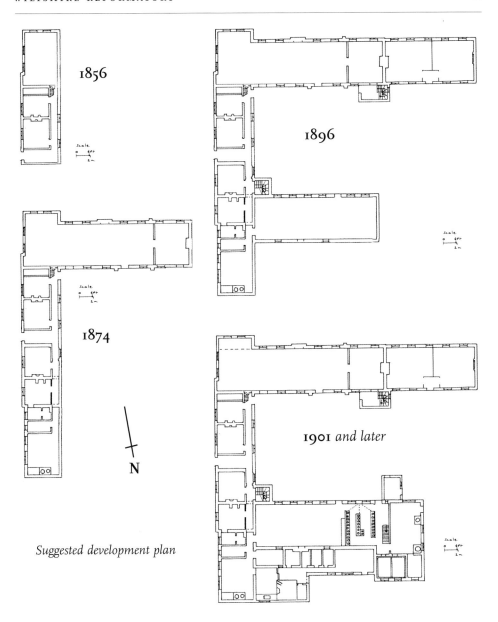

1856

1896

1874

N

Suggested development plan

1901 *and later*

accommodation was also increased by taking over the lease of a cottage near the school for the use of the farm labourer. In 1869 the cottage was improved so that it could act as a hospital for sick boys to be looked after by the labourer's wife.

The addition of the several wooden huts was clearly only a temporary and not entirely satisfactory arrangement but the committee was still concerned about their security of tender. But in 1873 White agreed that they could hold the lease for the remainder of his interest at a rent of £70 a year. Then Lord Bath promised that on the expiration of that interest he would grant a lease for 21 years at a fair agricultural value. The committee felt they now had sufficient security to invest in new buildings and Mr. Hardick was instructed to prepare plans at a cost of no more than £800. In February 1874 a tender was accepted from Mr. William Strong for £945, considerably more than originally intended, and the building was completed by October. The main east range was extended to the north and a new wing 45 feet by 20 feet was built on the south side. Altogether this provided on the ground floor a new schoolroom, bathroom and lavatory, a sitting room, tailor's shop, store room and three cells. On the first floor was a new dormitory, the schoolmaster's sitting room and bedroom. There were also three other bedrooms which could be used as sick rooms if necessary. A few years later there was felt to be a need for new bath accommodation so in 1881 a large cemented bath about 6ft. 6ins. square was built together with a dressing room with a movable partition at the west end of the schoolroom.

The next major development came in 1896 with a new dormitory on the site of existing outbuildings on the north side. The closets adjoining the bakehouse were also removed and replaced at the end of the new building. Mr. Ponton, a Warminster builder, submitted the lowest tender which the committee was inclined to accept but, after an unsatisfactory interview with him, they changed their minds and awarded the contract to Mr. Pearce who had submitted the second lowest tender. He agreed to reduce his

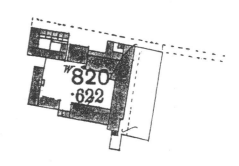

Ordnance Survey map showing the site in 1887 (WSRO)

original price of £342 by £12 but he was to be paid an additional £9 for moving the closets.

The last major extension was undertaken in 1901. Mr. H.C.M.Hirst, an architect from Bristol, was engaged to draw up plans to enlarge the school to take 100 boys. The new building had been expected to cost about £1200 but when Mr. Hirst presented his plan the estimate was nearer £1500. Hirst was engaged to supervise the work at a fixed fee of £60 but, if for any reason the scheme did not go ahead, he was to receive only 10 guineas for the work he had already done. There was a problem of getting a loan from the Capital and Counties Bank but this was solved when Mr. Cookson offered to lend the committee £1200 at 4% for the purpose of the building. The lowest tender was submitted by Butcher and Son of Warminster at £1550. The architect was instructed to amend the scheme to reduce the cost closer to his original estimate

Elevation of the south range from the north in 1953 with the 1874 section to the left and the 1896 addition to the right (WSRO)

otherwise the work would not be done. The committee eventually accepted the amended scheme and tender for £1319 14s. 3d. plus £33 for reconstruction of the boilers. This new work provided an enlargement of the schoolroom and two dormitories with new officers' rooms, laundry, drying room, baths, lavatory, kitchen, bakehouse, store room, larder, dairy and sick room.

A detailed description of the buildings was made by a reporter from the *Warminster and Westbury Journal* who visited the institution in June 1903. The buildings stood in neatly kept grounds, without a wall or high fence, and were in the shape of a square. The superintendent lived in the front or east side of the square and the school buildings stretched back from his house in two wings containing the schoolroom, dormitories and dining hall of the boys. On the other, west, side of the square was a building that had once been a barn but had been converted into a very nice day room at the end of which there was a stand of lockers, numbered, one for each boy. The schoolroom was a large, airy building well lighted and ventilated and altogether a cheerful looking place. In recent years some store rooms and cells had been demolished to make room for the main school building while a classroom for Standards I and II had been added by taking away a bathroom and boiler. New bathing accommodation had been provided in a new part of the institution. There were three dormitories: one above the schoolroom to accommodate 44 boys, another in the same building over the tailor's shop for 24 boys and the other for 34 boys on the opposite side of the square. The rooms of the masters were sandwiched very compactly so that there were always some of them in touch with the dormitories. On the same side of the square as the schoolroom was one of the most important and successful of the industrial departments, the tailor's shop. Next to this was the shoemaker's shop. The last, north side of the square had been only recently added. This contained a laundry with drying room attached and a smartly appointed lavatory with rows of iron basins fixed down the centre and around the sides. Behind were two cemented tanks for the Saturday night wash with hot and cold water which could be turned on at will. Upstairs there were some officers' rooms and another dormitory. Below this was the dining hall and then the bread store. The kitchen was rather smaller than might have been expected but there were plans to extend it when funds became available. It had a small cooking range but the bakehouse oven could also be used for roasting purposes and there was a capacious copper. Other small rooms included a lamp room, a potato store, a dairy and a room which the superintendent used to develop the 'fruits of his photographic expeditions'. The plans showing these alterations are in the Longleat archives. They show that the existing rooms at each end of the east range were taken up in height but most changes were to the north side of the courtyard. Finally in 1906 a campaign was started to raise money to build a gymnasium and sufficient money had been collected by 1909 to allow this to go ahead at a cost of £361.

The Reformatory had recurring problems with its water supply. For many years a well met all its needs but in 1889 the committee considered laying on piped water from the Warminster Local Board. Two routes for the pipe were examined: from the main road from Parrot's farm and across the fields in a

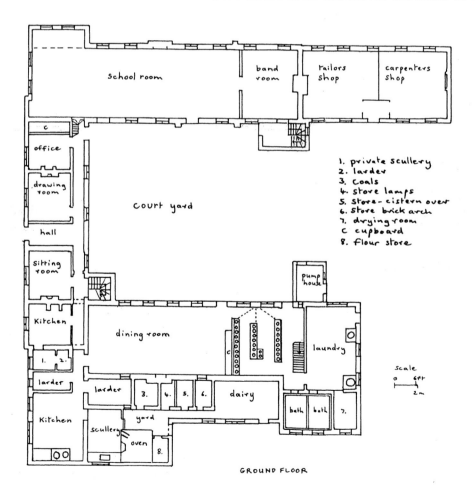

GROUND FLOOR

direct line to the Reformatory, a distance of 910 yards, but this would not pass near the hospital cottage; or through Bugley Farm and then to Sly's farm, a distance some 80 yards longer. The Local Board would lay the pipes using the labour of the boys. The Committee had long negotiations with the Local Board but could not agree a price for the work and decided to postpone the matter for a year. Then in May 1890 H.M. Inspector pointed out the absence of satisfactory arrangements in the case of fire and this, together with a report from the public analyst condemning the present water supply as unsatisfactory, forced the hand of the committee. They signed a contract with Mr. Long to lay a 3 inch main from Bugley to the Reformatory at a cost of £132 10s. In December 1890 they calculated that the Reformatory was using about 200 gallons of water a day and the cost for the first three months was between 17s. and 18s. The question of fire precautions arose again in 1898 when it was agreed to build a reservoir holding 1000 gallons to be placed on iron pillars near the baths. The mains water supply

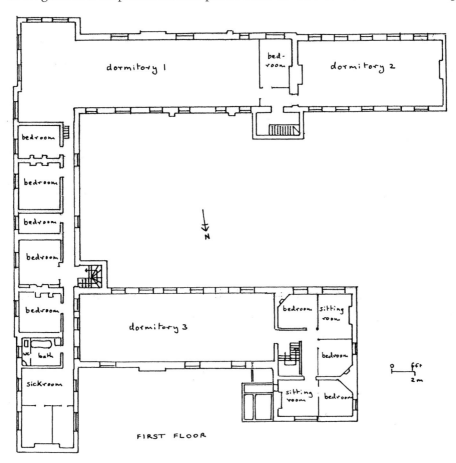

(Above and left) The Reformatory buildings in the final phase, based on architects' plans of 1901 (Longleat Estate) and 1953 (WSRO)

never seems to have been entirely satisfactory and there were frequent complaints about the lack of water. It became so bad that in December 1907 the committee decided to re-open the old well and to instal a 2 H.P. Hornsby pump and engine supplied by Reeves and Son of Bratton at a cost of £95. Although this gave an ample supply of water the old problem of contamination recurred and was the cause of an outbreak of goitre in the school. The committee then had to provide a 200 gallon tank fed from the town pipe to be used exclusively for drinking. The final problems came during the First World War when the additional demands from the army camps resulted in the supply virtually drying up. Once again they reverted to the old well although under close medical supervision.

The Staff

As Reformatories were so new it was very difficult in the early years to obtain staff who were experienced in the new approach to dealing with young offenders. This situation changed considerably in later years and, with a large number of Reformatories being established across the country, each institution could draw on a pool of qualified professional staff.

The manager and secretary to the committee was a part-time appointment and was always filled by a local vicar as an additional job. There were six holders of the post during the life of the Reformatory. Rev. Fane was succeeded in 1863 by Rev. Bob Hutton but he held the post for only two years. There then followed two managers who had perhaps the greatest influence on the development of the Reformatory: Rev. Jacob from 1866 to 1872 and Rev. Eliot, of Norton Bavant, from 1872 to 1891. The last two managers were Rev. Moore and Rev. Atwood.

The direct management of the Reformatory was led by the Superintendent. After Mr. White's dismissal in 1863 there were six holders of the post but two dominated by their length of service and their importance in establishing the national reputation of the Reformatory: Mr. Hendley (1863 to 1882) and Mr. Verity (1898 to 1920). Despite the misgivings about his military background, Mr. Hendley was responsible for putting the institution on a firm footing and in setting up an orderly regime. He saw the numbers double from about 25 to over 50 and he supervised the first major extension of the buildings in 1874. The H.M.Inspector reports from 1868 to 1877 give glowing accounts of the Reformatory and speak of the superintendent as being 'zealous and successful' and 'diligent and painstaking'. All this changed, however, from 1880 onwards when adverse comments began to creep into the reports about the well-being of the institution. Some cause for concern was noted by the committee in December 1881 and this was followed by a letter from H.M.

Inspector in April 1882 which expressed his concern about the state of the school and its discipline which 'gave rise to the question whether your superintendent owing to increase of years or growing infirmities or other causes is quite as efficient a man as he formerly was. We have a very great respect and regard for your superintendent. We have the highest opinion of his integrity and are quite sure that he is and always has been most anxious to do his duty. But we are anxious that the school should not suffer in its reputation.' There was also a suspicion that Mr. Hendley had starting drinking to excess. The committee decided that Mr. Hendley should be given a warning 'with regard to abstaining not only from what was bad in itself but from all appearance of what was bad and be cautioned with regard to attending more closely and personally to the management of the school.' Faced with these reports, Hendley said he intended to retire in December 1883 when he would have served for 20 years. But by July 1882 there was little change and Hendley resigned. He was given a quarter's salary from the date of his resignation and £8 for rations. He was also promised a gratuity of £25 at Michaelmas and a second gratuity of £25 at Lady Day 1863 provided he did not in any way interfere with the new superintendent but give advice and help if required.

The vacant post was advertised in the *Times, Standard* and *Daily Telegraph* at a salary of £100 a year with board and allowances. The standing of the Reformatory at that time was shown by the response from 400 applicants many of whom had good experience of Reformatory work. John Gill, assistant superintendent of the Suffolk Reformatory, was appointed but he stayed for only six years. Again there was an accusation of drunkenness this time from a Warminster tradesman with corroboration from some committee members. Gill resigned in 1888 and was replaced by Mr. Harold who, after three years, moved on to the Hampshire Reformatory. Mr. Walker from the Redhill Reformatory succeeded Gill and in 1898 he was promoted to be superintendent of the Leeds Reformatory.

Then came Mr. Verity who served the school with distinction for the next 22 years. He had worked in a certified school at Standen Bridge, Staffordshire and then at the Somerset Industrial School, Bath before becoming headmaster of Kingswood Reformatory School. He was described as a man of fine physique and of splendid character. While at Warminster he played an active part in the Freemasons' Lodge. The committee seems to have recognised the arduous nature of the job when in 1910 they voted him a grant of £10 towards the cost of a holiday on the condition that he went on a voyage. In 1912 a major review of salaries was undertaken including comparisons with other Reformatories. Verity and his wife were paid a basic salary of £140 but with allowances the total was calculated to be £239 9s. plus washing, fuel, light, milk, vegetables and the wage of a servant. He was given a £10 rise. Considerable problems were faced with the First World

War when it became very difficult to recruit staff at all levels. This may have been the start of his period of serious illness including an operation in the Warminster Cottage Hospital. An assistant superintendent was appointed to help him in 1919. Verity died in office in 1920. His funeral was attended by Lord Bath and about 100 boys from the Reformatory marched to the church. The final superintendent was Rev. Townson who had originally come to the Reformatory as head schoolmaster. His promotion coincided with his marriage which was essential as the superintendent's wife still had to act as matron.

The recruitment and retention of schoolmasters was much more difficult with most staying only for a few years. The post was hardly an attractive one. The holder, usually a single man, had to live in the Reformatory with his bedroom overlooking the boys' dormitory to enable him to supervise them. A list of the schoolmaster's duties in 1882 showed he had a very split day with teaching from 8 a.m. to 9 a.m. with a gap until 6 p.m. while the boys were out working. He then supervised the boys until 7 p.m. when he again taught them until 8.30 p.m. on four nights a week. He might be called upon for additional supervisory duties especially on wet days when the boys could not work. He was not allowed to leave the premises without permission although he could go out every Wednesday evening from dinner time until 10 p.m. As a general rule he was off duty alternate Saturdays from 6 p.m. to 10 p.m. and alternate Sundays except for 1½ hours Sunday School in the afternoon.

Several schoolmasters were dismissed for staying out all night in Warminster and for drunkenness which seems to have been prevalent amongst the staff. The first schoolmaster to be appointed when Hendley became superintendent was another army man, Corporal Gebbies of the Scots Fusiliers at a salary of 10s. a week, but he left four months later following a dispute with the superintendent. The next schoolmaster, Mr. Richmond White, came with strong recommendations from Manchester Training College but he was dismissed for staying out all night and for drinking until 3 a.m. In November 1880 Mr. Bamford was also charged with being drunk, with general misconduct and with being absent from duty despite repeated warnings. He was allowed to resign provided he left the premises within 24 hours. Two years later Mr. Sheaf was dismissed for exactly the same reasons culminating in his staying out all one night and then scaling the wall with a ladder to get back in. Some schoolmasters tried to take attention from their own shortcomings with accusations against the superintendent. Mr. Salmon's charge of drunkenness against Mr. Verity was found to be false and, as a consequence, he was dismissed.

The First World War presented its own problems of staff shortages. In November 1914 the head schoolmaster resigned presumably to join the armed forces. Successful appeals for exemption from conscription were made in 1916 on behalf of the new head schoolmaster and his assistant. These problems of recruitment and the general inflation led to significant increases in salaries so that by 1918 the head schoolmaster was earning £130 a year plus allowances and this was raised again in 1920 to £180 with annual increments of £10 to a maximum of £240 plus allowances. Perhaps the most successful appointment towards the end of the war was Rev. Townson. In 1919 he was promoted to be assistant superintendent because of Mr. Verity's state of health and in 1920, as we have seen, on Mr. Verity's death he became superintendent.

The committee sometimes struggled to maintain high standards in its officers. In October 1912 a visitor reported seeing officers unshaven and, as a result, it was ordered that every officer had to be shaved not later than 9 a.m. This problem must have been ongoing, for Rev. George Atwood in his diary for March 1915 recorded: 'This day found two Inspectors from the Education Department at the Reformatory, one unshaven, dirty rascal. How can I expect my officers to shave regularly if H.M.I.s don't!!!'

The other staff increased as the Reformatory expanded. At first the matron seems to have been directly responsible for all the domestic arrangements including the cooking although the boys helped with this and with the cleaning. The core of the institution, the farm and the agricultural training of the boys, was the responsibility of the labour master who had the help of one and later two labourers. From quite an early stage, shoemaking was an alternative to farming and a full time shoemaker, Mr. Applegate, was appointed in 1869. But in 1871 the committee received a letter from him to say that he had gone on holiday and intended to enlist as a soldier rather than return. He was followed by Mr. Wright, a master shoemaker, who stayed for 20 years and became one of the mainstays of the school. He was paid 10s. a week and lived in the 'hospital cottage' with his wife who took in and looked after any boy who became sick. When Mr. Wright retired through ill health he was given a gratuity of £25 but had to leave his cottage after a month. Tailoring was also an option for the boys and at first this was simply making shirts for the boys under the supervision of the matron. Later on a part-time tailor was appointed and the range of instruction extended. By 1910 the Reformatory also had a gym instructor, a band master, a part-time drill instructor, a cook, a laundress and a carpenter. The superintendent's wife was also given an allowance to pay for a maid servant.

The Boys and their Crimes

Unfortunately there is no register of the boys at the Reformatory or a record of their particular crimes. However, information can be obtained from the records of Quarter Sessions and Petty Sessions, newspaper reports, some national statistics and the minutes of the Reformatory Committee.

Almost without exception the boys sent to the Reformatory had been committed for stealing, often petty theft, although in 1901 the committee, having discussed one boy at the school, decided that in future they would not knowingly take any boy convicted of 'bestiality'. At first all the boys came from Wiltshire and the managers, always wanting to keep up numbers, complained if the magistrates sent a boy out-county. The first time this happened was in July 1883 when Richard Vallis was sent by the Warminster magistrates to Redhill because they thought the Wiltshire Reformatory was too near to his home. It occurred again in May 1884 when two brothers called Beer were convicted. The elder one was sent to Redhill and the younger, who the committee thought useless, went to Warminster.

The Reformatory very soon began to take in boys from outside the county, especially from Berkshire. In 1879 the Dorset Reformatory closed and from then on most of the boys convicted in Dorset were sent to Wiltshire. The number of out-county boys gradually increased until they formed well over half of the total number in the Reformatory. In 1866 of the 45 boys in the school, 19 came from Wiltshire, 5 from Berkshire, 8 from Bath and 3 from Exeter. By 1869 boys had also been admitted from Worcester and Middlesex. Thirteen years later only 16 of the 48 boys were from Wiltshire with 11 from Dorset, 6 from Bristol, 5 from Manchester, 4 from Devon, 3 from Berkshire, 2 from Bedford and 1 from Brecon. In 1894 the proportion of Wiltshire boys was even lower with only 19 out of a total of 63 with Dorset sending 13 and Southampton 10.

It is not always clear why magistrates sent some boys but not others to a Reformatory. The whole basis of the Reformatory was to reform boys who had been led into crime because of their home background. Some magistrates clearly had this in mind when they passed sentence and they also seemed to have taken previous convictions into account. However, others simply saw the Reformatory as a form of incarceration similar to a prison and stipulated a term of years based on the severity of the crime. The Reformatory committee consistently complained about this and insisted that they needed to have a boy for a full five years if they were going to achieve a successful outcome. They explained that if a boy was given only a three year sentence, he would complete it before he was old enough to support himself and would have to return to what often proved to be an unsuitable home. They gave an example of such a boy being found in rags, his mother having sold or pawned the two new suits of clothes and two new pairs of boots with which the Reformatory had fitted him out on his leaving the school.

The alternative punishments of gaol, whipping and fines continued. An analysis of the juvenile convictions in Wiltshire from 1871 to 1882 shows that only 17 % of the boys convicted were sent to a Reformatory while whipping remained the most common punishment.

Sentence	Number	%
Gaol	79	22
Gaol and whipping	36	10
Whipping	125	35
Fined	56	16
Reformatory	60	17
Industrial School	4	1

There was a much greater use of Reformatories with girls for whom whipping was not allowed.

Sentence	Number	%
Gaol	14	31
Fined	9	20
Reformatory	22	49

Of those 60 boys sent to the Reformatory 17 had been convicted for stealing sums of money ranging from 6d. to £2. Thirteen had stolen food, often very small amounts such as 2 eggs, 2lbs. of bread or a piece of bacon. Other offences might be regarded as quite minor such as stealing coal value 3d. or a piece of timber. The six who stole silver watches might perhaps have been more hardened criminals. The only crime not involving theft was the boy who threw stones at a luggage train.

The newspaper reports of trials at Quarter Sessions and Petty Sessions show a similar pattern. A significant number of those sent to the Reformatory had previous convictions or were known as difficult characters. James Slade and William Grant, both 15 from Malmesbury, each had two previous convictions. Charles Bell and Joseph Short of Salisbury, who were found guilty of stealing and of damaging the rifle butts of the First Wilts Rifle Volunteers at Laverstock, were said to have been several times convicted. A long history of problems surrounded William Scane (13). He had been sent by his father with 3½d. to buy some coal but he spent 1½d. on buns and chocolate and pocketed the other 2d. He then stole 38lbs. of coal. His mother said he had been giving her a lot of trouble, staying out at nights and not going regularly to school. He had previously been given three strokes of the birch for stealing. The home background was referred to in a number of cases. When Frank Winslow and Gilbert Saxby, both under 12, pleaded guilty to a long list of indictments charging them with stealing groceries, the chairman of Quarter Sessions felt obliged to administer a severe rebuke to the parents. The intention to use a Reformatory to remove a boy from an unsatisfactory home was clearly stated in the case of John Sly (13) who had been found guilty of throwing a stone at a younger boy. The chairman of Petty Sessions, noting that Sly was a very bad character, said the Bench considered his home surroundings and his chances in life were so bad that the best course would be to send him to a Reformatory for five years.

The boys, when charged, generally seem to have pleaded guilty and most accepted their sentence without demur. The exception was Walter Hervin (15) who was sentenced to five years in a Reformatory for stealing lead. 'The Bench made the order and immediately he heard it, the defendant made as if to take his coat off and offered to fight the magistrates who had sentenced him.' When Cecil Barclay (13) was convicted for stealing a penny and five packets of cigarettes, his father, a tanyard foreman, tried to argue against the Reformatory sentence on financial grounds. He said he had three children at home who did not bring in anything, three who brought in part of their keep, one was apprenticed, two were at home earning their own living and one was a soldier. His own average wage was 25s. a week and he could not afford to lose the money which Cecil had been earning. On one occasion the magistrates were seen to be much too harsh in using a previous conviction as the reason for a Reformatory sentence. George Hayward (14) was convicted of stealing a strap value 1s. A petition was signed by every adult male and female in Chitterne pointing out that the previous offence was committed when he was only seven and since then his conduct had been good. As a result, the Home Secretary advised remission of the Reformatory sentence. The journal *Truth* commented on 'Warminster Shallows, one of whom, as is usually the case when magistrates obtain unpleasant notoriety, is a beneficed clergyman of the Church of England.'

It would be wrong to suppose, however, that all the boys sent to the Reformatory were simply guilty of minor thefts caused by sheer deprivation and an unsatisfactory home background. Some were clearly hardened criminals who did not respond to attempts to reform them. In 1881 the directors of the Reformatory themselves brought a case against two 'incorrigibles' Henry Veale (16) and Albert Filer (17) for stealing a coat, waistcoat and a pair of trousers from an employee at the Reformatory. The directors said they had done so because of the extreme bad character of the two boys and the bad influence they exercised over their fellow inmates. Veale was given six months hard labour and Filer, who had been in prison on three previous occasions, got five years penal servitude.

The Reformatory Regime

For at least the first fifty years of its existence the Reformatory was run on very clear, strict principles. The key feature was simply hard work mainly through farming although a few were occupied in tailoring, shoemaking and, later, carpentry. Others were engaged in jobs around the Reformatory especially cleaning and cooking. The boys acquired their industrial training very much through practical working rather than any theoretical study. Basic education played a part but it seems to have been subsidiary to work and only later was it given a higher priority. The other basic aim was to keep the boys constantly occupied as a way of teaching them the merits of hard work and to avoid too much spare time which could tempt them into mischief or wrongdoing.

Farming was from the outset the main activity of the Reformatory. They started with 20 acres which seems to have been largely arable producing in 1863 wheat, barley, turnips, swedes, mangolds and potatoes. They also kept some pigs for in 1864 they installed new floors in the pigsties. A serious outbreak of swine fever occurred in 1885 and 47 pigs either died or had to be slaughtered. Other animals such as sheep and some cattle were gradually introduced. In 1868 they bought a horse in order to teach the boys the elements of horse management which would make them more useful to farmers. After ten years good service this horse had to be replaced because it was injured and was disfigured by large and numerous warts which refused to yield to any treatment. A new black gelding, rising four, was bought for £50 from a farmer in Chitterne. After 1900 the Reformatory concentrated on a herd of pedigree Jerseys. In June 1904 they sent to Warminster market a Jersey cow with her cross bred bull calf and told the auctioneer that they would be sending another shortly because they were overstocked.

With the agricultural depression in the 1880s the farm began to lose money despite the free labour of the boys and the managers considered giving up some of the land. This, however, did not happen and in 1902 they also took on 'Nutball Field' of 15 acres. Many of the boys were also employed under close supervision by neighbouring farmers and the money they earned helped to support the Reformatory. The managers realised the wisdom of not relying entirely on farming. At one stage it was simply a matter of finding enough work to keep the boys occupied and for this reason they started making faggots for fires. More importantly they extended the facilities for training in tailoring, shoemaking and carpentry. At first tailoring consisted of making clothes for the boys under the guidance of the matron. In 1863 they made 39 jackets, 50 pairs of trousers and 116 shirts. A part-time tailor was appointed in 1869 and the range of garments made was increased. Shoemaking was treated rather more seriously and a full time shoemaker became part of the Reformatory's staff. Again they started by making and repairing boots for the boys (76 pairs in 1863) but this was extended to outside work including making 'slippers' for the Warminster maltsters. In 1889 7 of the 61 boys in the school were engaged in tailoring, 5 in shoemaking, 2 helped with the cooking and 4 with cleaning. The remainder worked on the farm. Carpentry became very successful and the school was presented with a lathe by the Company of Turners. In 1923 two boys, Charles Oakley and Henry Hartley, won first and second prizes for wood turning in a competition open to all schools in the country.

It was commonly recognised in the 19th century that criminal activity amongst juveniles and a lack of educational achievement were closely linked. National statistics for 1895 show that only about 14% of boys and girls admitted to Reformatories could read and write adequately.

	Cannot read or write	Read and write imperfectly	Read and write well	Superior
Boys	126	691	124	9
Girls	32	112	20	—
	158	803	144	9

No comparable statistics are available for the Wiltshire Reformatory but of the 90 juveniles convicted in Wiltshire between 1871 and 1882 who were required to sign a document, 68 (76%) managed a signature and 22 (24%) made a mark. The H.M. Inspector in his report on the Reformatory in 1873 commented that the class of boys from which the school was recruited was not very intelligent.

The education classes were held early in the morning before the boys began their farm work and again in the early evening when they returned probably very tired. This arrangement could hardly have been conducive to concentration. Despite this, the boys do seem to have made some progress at least in the basics of reading and writing. The importance of religion in the foundation of the Reformatory was reflected in the teaching of Religious Knowledge alongside the three Rs. In 1874 the Inspector reported that the educational achievements had improved compared with former years; the lowest classes had been well attended to and the ciphering and dictation of the upper classes was very creditable. Two years later they were continuing to make progress although their dictation and oral spelling were indifferent and their copy writing only fair. In 1880 the boys passed the Inspector's examination very well, their work being unusually correct and neatly done throughout. In the 1st class of 13 boys, 32 sums out of 39 set were correctly answered in practice, proportions and bills of parcel; in the 2nd class of 18, 17 dictations were correct but only 42 of the 54 sums. By 1902 there were 102 boys in the school and, of these, 14 had reached the highest Standard VI, 15 were in Standard V, 26 in Standard IV, 21 in Standard III, 13 in Standard II and 12 in Standard I. All were described as 'good'.

After the First World War, the government adopted new policies which gave greater weight to education than to the older industrial training through practical work. As part of this move, the government proposed that Reformatories should no longer be responsible solely to the Home Office but there should be Dual Control by the Home Office and the Education Department. This was hotly opposed by Reformatory managers and Wiltshire's Rev. Atwood was part of the deputation which went to the Home Office to protest strongly. This does not seem to have been successful and Atwood was not impressed by the Home Office minister Mr. Griffiths, whom he described as 'a dxxxd Radical and a Welshman!' In 1919 the Home Office issued specific instructions to the Wiltshire Reformatory which had to be followed if the variable grant was to be awarded. Boys under 14 had to spend their core time of five hours a day in school classes rather than in working on the farm and backward boys over that age were also to be kept in school if necessary. Boys over 14 were to receive part-time education with eight hours a week on school work at times when they were not likely to be physically tired. The industrial side also had to change with a greater emphasis on instruction. In farming, for example, there had to be teaching of skilled work and lectures had to be given on the work of the day. In tailoring the boys had to learn a greater range of skills, making actual suits of clothes as opposed to uniform. The salaries of the teachers needed to be raised in order to attract better qualified staff and no class was to exceed 16 in number. It seems likely that the Reformatory had some difficulty in adapting its long traditions and practices to meet the new requirements.

The main punishments used in the Reformatory were periods of isolation in a cell, restriction on food and the infliction of strokes with a birch. There is a peculiar reference in the committee minutes in 1880 to two steel collars which had been made some 15 years previously to fasten on the neck of any unusually bad boy especially when absconding was involved. Although the collars never seem to have been used, the Manager felt he should seek the advice of H. M. Inspector. There was a somewhat horrified reply saying that on no account should they ever be used. In 1883 the committee agreed a more formal set of rules about discipline and punishments. The superintendent was authorised to use the birch or cane but six strokes was the maximum he could give without the special sanction of the Manager. All punishments of six cuts or less had to be reported to the Manager. The superintendent could also on his own authority confine a boy to the cells for up to 36 hours but it was understood that, as a rule, he was not to give more than 24 hours with an extra 12 hours only if he could not find the Manager at home to approve it. Any boy confined to a cell for more than 48 hours had to be seen at once by a doctor. The labour masters were allowed to carry a cane and, if they considered it necessary, administer one or at the outside two sharp cuts to any refractory boy.

On the opening of the Reformatory in 1856 it was decided that the boys' clothing should include a waistcoat, two pairs of corduroy trousers and a smock frock with some distinctive mark. The wearing of a uniform was intended to help the boys associate with the institution and, very practically, to allow a boy to be easily recognised if he absconded. It is not certain exactly what the uniform looked like but it seems to have included a red stripe which was later abolished. In 1884 there was a discussion about hats for the boys and it was eventually decided that they should have a hat for Sundays and on the other days of the week they would have a kind of Scotch cap. The Annual Report for 1905 records the full outfit issued to a boy on admission to the Reformatory and the set of clothes he was given when he was discharged. On admission he received 1 Bedford cord suit, 1 corduroy suit, 1 black cloth cap, 1 cord cap, 2 regatta shirts, 2 flannel shirts, 2 night shirts, 2 pairs of woollen socks, 2 pairs of boots, 1 pair of gaiters, 2 kerchiefs, 1 pair of braces, 2 towels and 1 bath towel. The 'wardrobe' he had on discharge must have made him quite well dressed compared with many of his contemporaries: 2 suits of clothes, 2 hats or caps, 4 collars and fronts, 1 tie, 2 shirts, 3 pairs of socks, 2 pairs of boots, 1 pair of braces, 4 kerchiefs, 2 woollen vests, 1 box, a Bible and a prayer book. Uniform was abolished in 1921 on the grounds of economy and the boys then wore plain clothes with a distinctive badge on the cap and shoulder.

The boys seem to have been given a strict but simple diet which in 1856 was said to be based on the Gloucester scale as far as circumstances permitted. It is not clear exactly what this was but some indication of the meals provided can be gleaned from later decisions about changes to the diet. In 1872, for example, it was decided to offer each boy a pint of coffee or cocoa for supper, to take away the butter from breakfast and to give suet pudding and treacle on Wednesdays instead of soup for dinner. The Manager was given discretion in 1879 to allow the boys a fish dinner from time to time but this was not to happen more than once a week. A good indication of the overall diet can be gained from the tender put out for the supply of certain items of food for the six month period from 1 October to 31 March 1880:

> Bacon, American 600lbs, cheese 300lbs, cheese, better quality 120lbs, butter, salt, 3rd. cork 250 lbs, lard, foreign 60lbs, coffee, in berry 80lbs, sugar, moist 1000lbs, sugar, loaf 72lbs, flour, good seconds 40 bags, beef, flanks without bone 320lbs, joints, beef or mutton 520lbs, suet 260lbs.

It is noticeable that the items are not of the top quality and, although the amounts seem large, it would be on average only 4½lbs meat, 3½lbs bacon and 2lbs of cheese a day for 50 boys and the staff. They would have had their home-grown vegetables and they baked their own bread. A further indication is the 'special' meal provided at the harvest supper in 1906: 'leg of mutton, potatoes, parsnips followed by plum puddings, a solid two pound cut popped on each plate.'

Absconding

Most of the boys seem to have accepted their sentence to a Reformatory and many gained a lot from it, eventually appreciating the new start in life it had given them. But others did not accept the strict routine and absconding was a constant problem. The absconding was almost always associated with other crimes, particularly stealing. The first thing that the boys had to do after absconding was to steal some clothes to replace their uniform and then to find food. Even so, most were caught within a few days not least because there was a reward of £1 for capturing and returning an escaped Reformatory boy. On being caught, the boys were then charged with the criminal offences both of absconding and stealing.

In 1882, for example, three boys Henry Henstridge, Henry Hibberd and Daniel Gibbs absconded after dinner. They stole two jackets from two labourers but were found by P.C. Hayter in a shed at about 2 a.m. They still had on their Reformatory clothes but with the stripes cut out of their trousers. Henstridge and Hibberd were each given three months hard labour for absconding and all three got a month's hard labour for stealing. Another group of Reuben Thornton (14), John Williams (16), George Williams (13) and James Lush (13) got almost to Salisbury before being caught. They made for Cley Hill, then Westbury and slept for part of the night under a rick at Imber. They then made their way towards Salisbury but were spotted by a carter and two shepherds. They were enticed into the shepherd's hut on the promise of some clothing but the shepherds locked them in.

Most of the abscondings involved a group or pair of boys and were pre-planned. In 1910 Joseph Harris suggested to Eli Hill that they should run away. He first stole £6 or £7 in gold and silver and a card case from the desk of Mr. Salmon, the master. They left on Saturday 29 January at 4.30 p.m. and went through some woods to a village where they bought some cakes for 2s. They slept the night in Mr. Allard's shed and on Sunday morning took the road to Gillingham arriving there at about 2 p.m. Later in the evening a policeman spotted them and managed to capture Hall but Harris got away. They were wearing old hats and overcoats over their Reformatory uniform. Harris was later caught, still with the card case but by then he had only £2 15s. 6d. left.

Some acted on their own and repeated the offence. Charles Rhodes had been sentenced at Bath in 1888 to five years in a Reformatory for stealing a pot of marmalade. He had previously spent five years in an Industrial School. He made his escape while out working in a group of nine boys under the supervision of the labour master. He was eventually caught in Salisbury and sent back to the Reformatory but absconded again in May. The Manager said he was one of the most troublesome and worst boys they had ever had and that he had been punished frequently for insubordination. He was sentenced at Quarter Sessions to three months' imprisonment and then to return to the Reformatory.

Some boys managed to get back to their home where they were abetted by their family. Alfred Chorley, for example, absconded and got to Bath where his mother lived. She gave him fresh clothes and started him off to his uncle in London but, on arriving there, his uncle immediately handed him over to the Bow Street police. Occasionally a boy was never re-captured. Joseph Short absconded in December 1871. He had been confined to a cell for theft but had managed to take the hinges off the door during the night. Nothing was heard of him until nearly a year later when he was sighted near his father's house. The police again failed to apprehend him but his father George Short, a shoemaker, was charged with harbouring him and assisting his concealment.

The boys often gave as an excuse for their absconding their dislike of the Reformatory and their treatment there. Alfred Chapman declared: 'I don't like it there and I am not going to stay there. They don't give me enough food and I shall never stop there.' Nothing was gained from absconding for the usual punishment was a month or so in prison and then return to the Reformatory to complete their sentence to which was added the time they were in prison.

Health

The annual reports generally said that the boys were in good health. But it was obvious that some had quite serious weaknesses when they were admitted and the great fear of any institution was that there would be an outbreak of an infectious disease.

The first death of a boy to occur at the Reformatory was William Edwards aged 11 in 1878. The cause of death was not stated but he was said to have received careful nursing and every attention from the Reformatory staff. In the next year there were three deaths but again the Medical Officer reported that these resulted from old standing complaints and had nothing directly or indirectly to do with the Reformatory. In 1881 a boy named Sturges died and there was a strong rumour that he had been poisoned through eating the leaves of the plant Lords and Ladies but a post mortem showed this not to be the case and he had died of inflammation of the lungs.

The great fear of a serious infectious disease was realised in 1887 with the outbreak of scarlet fever. This started with the daughter of Mrs. Gill, the matron, and unfortunately she died. Then one boy caught it and he was moved to the

Infectious Hospital at Warminster Common. By early 1888 there had been altogether six cases, one of which had proved fatal. Scarlet fever broke out again in the autumn with two boys being taken ill. The outbreak died down towards the end of the year and had disappeared altogether by February 1889. This episode caused the committee to look again at its arrangements for sick boys especially if they had an infectious disease. A formal agreement was drawn up with the Wrights who lived in the 'hospital' cottage.

They were to live there rent free and Mrs. Wright was to be paid 6d. a day for each sick boy she nursed. If an epidemic occurred, she would have to make arrangements to send her own children away to make room for the sick boys. Also, if any of her children caught a contagious or infectious disease, they would be removed immediately to the Warminster Infectious Hospital.

In 1896 there was an epidemic of boils which was blamed on the overcrowding in the dormitories made worse by the indiscriminate use of towels. The great influenza outbreak in 1918-19 also affected the school but there were no deaths or complications.

Harvest Homes and other Celebrations

The annual harvest home celebration established itself as the most important event in the school's calendar with all the resemblance of a school Speech Day. In 1868, for example, work for the day was suspended and, although it was fairly wet, there was a programme of outdoor sports. The games included picking up 50 stones placed a yard apart, three flat races over 200 yards, three wheelbarrow races with the runners blindfolded, three jingling matches, two three-legged races, three hurdle races, two sack races and three long jumps. There was also scrambling for apples and these 'disappeared with the rapidity of magic'. The boys then adjourned to the schoolroom which had been beautified with flags, festoons of flowers and miniature sheaves of corn. A number of short plays and recitations were performed by the boys and then they sang harvest hymns and God Save the Queen. Finally the supper: 'They fell to with a will and ate with such an unappeasable appetite as only boys who are growing and accustomed to hard work and plain fare could show!' This became the standard pattern for the day but from the 1870s onwards the Manager reported on the year's work and there was a visiting preacher usually from one of the local villages.

Some parents attended but perhaps they were embarrassed by the Manager, Rev. Eliot, when he declared that 'the school supplied the place of that care, attention and training which had not been given by drunken parents, by harsh step-parents or had been neglected by or misapplied by foolish, overindulgent parents'. Some old boys of the Reformatory also put in an appearance and as these were usually the successful ones, they were held up as good examples: 'Their presence on such occasions, respectfully dressed and well behaved as they always are, cannot but have good effect on those still undergoing detention by letting them see that a bright future is also in store for them if they only do their duty and conform to the high principles which are inculcated at the school.' The visiting preacher inevitably addressed his homily to the boys, stressing the importance of morality and of a Christian education. Rev. Powell of Sutton Veny in 1878 referred to the Reformatory as being 'founded upon the most Christian of all Christian principles, that of a return from evil to good, from misery to happiness' and he impressed on the boys 'the advantages which they enjoyed as having regular, systematic and healthy employment, a good secular education fitting them for any position in future life to which they are likely to be called, a sound religious education and a general moral training for good the whole of their future lives'. Unsurprisingly it was the special meal which the boys most enjoyed as in 1904: 'The plates, heaped with a dinner that might have satisfied that American who has just died of overeating, were soon emptied.'

By 1900 the Reformatory also had an annual outing to Shearwater and a sports day. The boys, headed by the band, marched to the lake where they had some boats, had tea and then sang several songs and glees. The sports day in 1903 was attended by Lady Bath and others from Longleat House including the Duchess of Somerset, Viscount Weymouth, Ladies Violet and Emma Thynne and Miss Rachel Thynne. Lady Bath said it was her first visit to the Reformatory but she had always been struck by the order, discipline and good behaviour of the boys when they had come to Longleat.

It was about this time that Lord and Lady Bath provided a Christmas treat for the boys at Longleat. In 1909, for example, they marched away from the school at 2.45 with the band and arrived at Longleat at 4 p.m. Tea was served in the servants' hall while the officers were entertained separately by Lord and Lady Bath and their guests. The evening concluded in the great hall with entertainment by Fred Vallance, a conjuror from Bristol. At 7.30 p.m. each boy received an orange before forming up and marching back to the Reformatory.

Special Incidents

There is a story related by the present inhabitants of Tascroft that a boy committed suicide in the tailor's shop and that his ghost still haunts the premises. There is, however, no documentary evidence of any such suicide although Daniel Gibbs (17) did make an unsuccessful attempt on his own life in 1882. He had been put in the cells after stealing a handkerchief from and threatening Mr. Hendley the superintendent. Mr. Wright went to take him for exercise on Tuesday morning and found the boy lying on his side, his head drooping and a brace tied round his neck. Luckily he was found in time and was revived. He was charged in the police court with attempting to commit suicide and with stealing. The suicide charge was dismissed but he was given a month's hard labour for stealing.

Much more serious was the incident in August 1882 when Frank Dance aged 13 was shot and killed. William Baverstock (16) and Frank Dance had been given the job of cleaning the labour master's room. There they found a gun which the labour master kept for shooting birds. At first Baverstock said that he had not touched the gun and that Dance had shot himself. He later changed his story and explained that they did not know that the gun was loaded and had larked around with it. Then Dance enticed him into pulling the trigger, the gun went off and Dance was shot in the back of the head. The inquest decided that the death was caused by misadventure and without malice but they censured the labour master for keeping a loaded gun in his room. Baverstock had to face trial and the magistrates taking into account his age and the fact that he and Dance were friends, dismissed the case with a caution.

The Reformatory and Relations with Warminster

The Wiltshire Reformatory was, in origin, closely linked with Warminster. It was often referred to as the Warminster Reformatory and the founder, Rev. Fane, and subsequent managers all came from Warminster or one of the surrounding villages. Yet for most of the first 30 years or so of its existence the Reformatory had only very limited contact with the town. This was partly because of the Reformatory's physical separation, being two miles away in the middle of fields, and partly from the Reformatory's policy of confining the boys within the institution except when they were working under close supervision on neighbouring farms. In the early years the boys seem to have been marched to church in Warminster on Sundays but this stopped when numbers became too large. The masters also went into Warminster on their evenings off but the number of incidents of heavy drinking could hardly have enhanced the reputation of the Reformatory. Local traders won contracts to supply the Reformatory with foods and other goods. For example, in 1880, the Reformatory accepted tenders from Mr. Brodribb for groceries, Miss Langley for meat, Messrs. Hurrell and Baker for clothing, Mr. Harris for flour and Mr. Stevens for coal, all of whom had their businesses in the Warminster area. The

Old postcard of the period 1909-24, showing the main, east, elevation and the gymnasium to the right (Warminster History Society)

determination of the committee to keep the boys away from the local population is shown by their reaction to the invitation from the town for the boys to join in with their celebration of the Queen's Jubilee in 1887. The committee considered it inadvisable to allow the boys to join with others and to be in the town late at night. Instead they made their own arrangements for a dinner of roast beef and plum puddings followed by a sports programme. The only concession was to allow the older boys to watch the distant firework display from their dormitory windows. The committee were equally concerned about keeping local residents, or at least the undesirable ones, away from the Reformatory. Thus in 1882 they sought an assurance from Messrs. Jupe, owners of the silk winding mills, that they would undertake to prevent as far as possible their factory girls from being a nuisance to the Reformatory.

It was only after 1900 that the Reformatory adopted a more liberal and outward looking policy. A major factor in this was the formation of the Reformatory Band which staged an annual concert at The Athenaeum and which became an important event in the Warminster calendar. The *Warminster and Westbury Journal* advertised and later reviewed the concert held in April 1902. The advertisement (which pre-dated modern concepts of political correctness) promised a 'Grand Evening of Minstrel ENTERTAINMENT with Niggers! Niggers! Niggers!' The programme would consist of 'coon' songs, plantation melodies and choruses, jokes, conundrums, stump speeches and comical sketches. In the interval 16 boys gave an exhibition of physical drill under the direction of Sergeant Major Taylor. Reserved seats cost 3s., second seats 2s., admission 1s. and under the gallery 6d. In commenting on the success of the concert, the editor also had high praise for the Reformatory and its management: '. . . the evidences there were of the excellence of the present regime of the Reformatory. The iron had not entered into the soul of any of the boys there. Had the performance been given by a high-class private school, the lads could not have been better behaved, more hearty or more willing. All looked well fed, well cared for and happy . . . and succeeds in fact in providing a class of boy who is even superior to the ordinary boy whose parents are of the labouring class'.

The Reformatory also formed its own football team and played a series of friendly games against local teams although they always played at home and were not allowed to play away. In October 1909, for example, the team was beaten by 5 goals to 3 by Warminster Christ Church and this was reported as their first defeat of the season. In the following year they played such teams as St. Boniface's College, Warminster St. John's and Corsley. The 1911 season was less successful with a 6–0 defeat by Warminster Reserves with the press report revealing a less than perfect Reformatory pitch: '. . . the school kicked down the slope!' Cricket was played but was less prominent although in July 1914 they did play and lose to Longleat by 70 runs to 47.

The aims and strategies of the Reformatory movement in attempting to reform convicted juveniles compared with the prison system was the subject of a lengthy discussion at the Warminster Literary and Debating Society in 1906. Mr. Verity, the superintendent, spoke on 'the principles and results of the movement' and Mr. Jones explained the main features of the prison system. Verity outlined the approach taken by the Reformatory, emphasising the importance of gaining the boys' confidence, making up for lost education, putting religion as the basis for all actions and getting boys physically fit. Somewhat more controversial were his comments about getting the boys used to hard work: 'One of the greatest difficulties to contend with is the boy's antipathy, at first, to steady and constant employment. He comes principally from the casual labourer classes who are quite content with a little work now and then but who object to it as a regular thing'. Jones, by contrast, explained that the prison system was inevitably based more on punishment and deterrents than reform: 'In youth the deterrent effects of punishment are small and the beneficial effects of Reformatory measures are at their maximum; in manhood this condition of things is reversed and the deterrent effects of punishment exceed the beneficial effects of reformative influences.' In the debate which followed 'it was generally acknowledged that the Reformatory system was undoubtedly the best method of dealing with juvenile offenders and had yielded most beneficial results but the pros and cons of the application of the same principle to the treatment of adult criminals was keenly debated.'

Successes, Failures and Finance

The Reformatory's progression was not always a smooth or steady one. There was the crisis, mainly financial and administrative, when Rev. Fane retired in 1863. There was also the decline and problems towards the end of Mr. Hendley's long period as superintendent in 1882. Lack of sufficient numbers threatened the financial viability of the institution in 1892 and the manager felt it necessary to write to the governors of the gaols in neighbouring counties to try to persuade them to send boys to the Wiltshire Reformatory. By the end of the year there appeared to be an annual deficit of about £100 and this caused sufficient concern for the manager to inform the Home Secretary in January 1893 of the intention to close the Reformatory at midsummer unless the position improved. Fortunately numbers picked up and the committee withdrew the notice of closure.

Generally, however, the Reformatory got glowing annual reports from H.M. Inspector and established itself as one of the leading institutions in the country. The main criterion for measuring success or failure was the proportion of leavers who did well after departing from the Reformatory and were not re-convicted. National league tables were published based on the previous three years' leavers. In many years the Wiltshire Reformatory recorded that about 90% were doing well and only, on average, were 10% re-convicted:

	Success rate %	Position in national league table
1857	88	2
1868	88	2
1869	96	1
1870	91	2
1871	91	1
1872	90	5
1873	93	2

In 1875 Wiltshire was third with 94%, behind Suffolk and Old Mill (Aberdeen) who both scored 96%

It was important that those discharged should not only not re-offend but also obtain steady employment. Finding suitable employers was a constant problem for the Reformatory and the annual report for 1865 contained a plea for help: 'Your Committee have endeavoured, as far as they could, to obtain situations for each boy as he leaves. This has been found impossible in all cases . . . It would be a great assistance to the committee if any who have the means of finding employment . . . would from time to time communicate with the Manager on the subject.' Of the 22 leavers in 1863, 2 enlisted in the army, 2 went to sea, 3 got jobs in private domestic service, 3 were employed as shoemakers and 2 as tailors, 4 became shop or errand boys, 1 was in the Salisbury workhouse, 1 was still looking for employment and 1 had been sentenced to penal servitude. Again in the period 1897-8-9, 61 boys were discharged: 35 into regular employment, 5 in casual employment, 16 enlisted in the army, 1 was unknown and 4 were re-convicted. The number of boys joining the army or navy seems to have increased dramatically towards the end of the century and this may be connected with the Boer War. In 1894-5-6, 4 boys enlisted in the army and 3 in the navy. After 1900 a significant number of the leavers joined the armed services:

	Leavers	Army	Navy
1902-4	67	8	4
1903-5	88	20	1
1908-10	89	25	—
1910-12	92	22	1

Other boys went to sea in merchant ships rather than in the navy. For example, Swift and Bell were sent to sea as apprentices at a cost of £7 each and two old boys, A. E. Slade and R. G. Ayling, were amongst the seamen lost in the Titanic disaster.

The other solution was to assist suitable boys to emigrate, mainly to Canada. The first report of such an emigration was in 1869 when it was agreed that Charles Tanner and John Harper could go to Canada. A year later it was reported that Tanner was doing well. In 1873 the committee justified its decision to give financial assistance to boys to emigrate rather than to return to undesirable homes: 'They had on that account felt themselves justified in allowing several to emigrate notwithstanding the expense which had thus been incurred and hitherto that had proved entirely successful'. The annual report for 1872 said that 15 boys had already been sent to Canada and all were doing well. There were some strings attached for the boys had to promise to try to make a success of their new country and not to consider returning home for at least four years: 'That in consequence of the kindness shewn and the expense incurred by the committee they were not to think of returning to England until they had been at least four years in Canada and had honestly tried to make their way there.' A few went to Australia but this seems not to have been as successful as Canada. Of the leavers in 1872-4, two went to Australia but one returned to England and was then sent to prison while the other was thought to have died but was later found and was doing well.

The Reformatory was never far away from financial problems. It was started as a voluntary project and sufficient money was raised by contributions from the 'great and the good' across Wiltshire to pay for the original building.

There was also no great problem in raising £284 in 1863 to pay off the outstanding debt and allow the Reformatory to make a fresh start. On that occasion the donations included £25 from the Marquis of Westminster, £12 from the Marquis of Ailesbury, and £10 each from Sir E. Antrobus, T. Baring M.P., Earl Nelson and Rt. Hon. T. Estcourt. The main building extensions in 1874 and 1901 were funded partly by donations and partly by loans. It was much more difficult, if not impossible, to get sufficient annual subscriptions to maintain the institution. For the first ten years of the Reformatory the annual income came mainly from the Treasury which had been authorised to make grants to certified Reformatories by the 1854 Act. This was supplemented by the profits from the farm and the hiring out of the boys to neighbouring farmers. During the crisis of 1863 the committee had a lengthy discussion about alternative methods of funding but they were determined to try to maintain their independence and continue to manage on the government grant and voluntary subscriptions. But a renewed appeal produced promises amounting to only £42 a year. The committee was therefore forced in 1865 to apply to the county, i.e. the Quarter Sessions. They agreed to pay 4s a week plus £2 for clothing on entry for every boy sent to the Reformatory. This was reduced to 2s. a week in 1870 when the finances were more healthy. These grants continued and were taken over by the new County Councils after 1880. Income became increasingly dependent on the number of boys at the institution and any decrease in numbers threatened financial disaster as in 1892. The Reformatory also suffered during the 1880s when the agricultural depression affected all farming profits.

The summary accounts for 1880 and 1905 show the main items of income and expenditure and the changes which were occurring:

	1880	1905
Income		
Treasury grant	961 15 3	1576 1 7
County and borough	327 9 6	682 14 7
Hire of boys	196 9 7	119 3 7
Farm	432 2 4	292 1 0
Other	13 12 6	
Overdrawn/balance	117 4 7	133 7 2
	2048 13 9	2803 7 11
Expenditure		
Salaries	279 0 2	451 19 4
Provisions	578 13 9	764 15 2
Clothing	100 19 11	139 11 5

Fuel,repairs,rates	135 16 7	294 16 6
Other	263 12 3	405 11 0
Rent	92 0 0	60 0 0
Farm	426 10 5	407 16 0
Repayment of loan		250 0 0
Overdrawn/balance	172 0 8	28 18 6
	_____	_____
	2048 13 9	2803 7 11

Income from the counties in 1905 was double that in 1880 because of the increase in the number of boys but the main income was still the Treasury grant – 47% of income in 1880 and 56% in 1905. The farm just about broke even in 1880 but it seems to have made a loss in 1905. In the 1880 accounts, £170 of the farm income was the notional value of vegetables and other food provided to the Reformatory. It was clear that at least by 1900 the Reformatory's future lay entirely in the hands of the government and this was to be the deciding factor when closure came in 1924.

Closure

The closure of the Reformatory by the Home Office in 1924 came with very little warning. The problems of the First World War, especially staff shortages, had been successfully weathered although perhaps the Reformatory found it more difficult to accommodate all the liberal changes required by the Home Office in 1919. Apart from the education changes, the Reformatory was required to abolish uniform and relax its discipline, for example by allowing the boys to run as they liked to the sports field instead of being marched there. Seaside camps had to be established and each boy had to spend a week every year in one of them. The boys were also to receive a third of all their earnings.

Yet the committee was still full of confidence. Rev. Townson was appointed superintendent in 1920 on the death of Mr. Verity but the new headteacher, Mr. Bird, proved to be

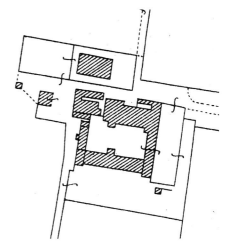

Ordnance Survey map showing the site in 1924 (WSRO)

The buildings from the north-west today. The attached single storey scullery, store rooms and dairy have gone.

unsuccessful and was forced to leave in 1921. His replacement, Mr. Albury, lasted only a few months because, being married, he refused to live on the school premises. The committee even considered plans in 1921 for some ambitious improvements and additions to the building. These had to be scaled down in view of the estimated cost of £9,000 to £10,000. Instead they looked to erect permanent offices and then buy three ex-army huts for a recreation room, cowshed and cart shed. Unfortunately suitable army huts were no longer available and the whole scheme fell through.

The real problem, however, was the acute financial problems of the 1920s. The government was forced to make severe cuts in public expenditure and in 1922 required the committee to reduce its staffing costs by £160, suggesting that Winter, the cook, and Farrer, the gym instructor, be dismissed. The committee particularly wanted to keep Farrer so they replaced Winter with a cook residing on the premises and dismissed Rickard, the shoemaker. Farrer was retained as part-time gym instructor and part-time shoemaker. Even with these early warnings, the closure seems to have come out of the blue. In January 1924 a special meeting was called to consider a letter from the Home Office to Lord Bath. The minutes of the meeting recorded: 'For reasons set forth in the letter, the Secretary of State proposed that the school should be closed and asked the committee whether any objections to this course would be raised.'

Unfortunately that letter is not in the records but the *Warminster Journal* was in no doubt that the reasons were purely financial ones: 'We learn that the Wiltshire Farm School [*sic*] will be closed within three months. For some time the government in its efforts to economise has been closing industrial schools and schools of the same category as the Wiltshire Farm School but the news that this local institution has been caught in the economy net will be learnt with regret locally.' The surprising thing is that the committee seems to have accepted this without a murmur. After some discussion it was proposed by Lord Heytesbury and seconded by Canon Jacob 'That the committee accepts the decision of the Secretary of State as expressed in his letter to the Marquess of Bath dated 7th January 1924 to close the school and that the committee is prepared to cooperate with the Home Office in carrying out the necessary arrangements.' No new boys were to be admitted and all the staff were given three months' notice. It is not clear what happened to all the boys but 39 were transferred to the Weston Training Board.

A formal notice of closure appeared in the press in May 1924 when all creditors and others having claims on the committee were asked to submit their accounts. The notice stated that the committee would then proceed to distribute the assets of the Reformatory 'amongst the parties entitled thereto'. There is, unfortunately, no record of what the Trustees did with all the contents of the Reformatory or how they disposed of any money remaining after the creditors were paid.

Inside the courtyard today looking towards the rear of the main, east, range

The land at Tascroft was only held on lease from Lord Bath and this was due in any case to expire at the end of September 1924. Thus the land and all the buildings on it simply reverted to Lord Bath. As well as this, the committee had to meet the cost of a list of dilapidations prepared by the Longleat Estate estimated to be £441 7s. 6d. Tascroft then became a farm with the front range serving as the farm house and the rest of the building becoming store rooms. This continued until 1953 when Lord Bath through the architect G. Blair Imrie obtained planning permission to convert the buildings into 13 separate dwellings. Some of the peripheral buildings including some of the farm buildings were knocked down. The development was undertaken by T. Holdoway and Sons of Westbury. The Tascroft complex remains today in that form comprising a farm and apartments mainly let to employees and ex-employees of the Longleat Estate.

The missing building is the gymnasium. In 1930 Lord Bath, in memory of his wife Violet, erected a new village hall at Horningsham to replace a converted army hut. It was designed by Captain Edmond Warre, a London architect, and built by Messrs. R. Butcher and Son. Most of the building materials came from the Reformatory gymnasium and the village hall still retains many of the features of that building.

Appendix
Reformatory for Girls at Limpley Stoke

A reformatory for girls was opened in 1861 at Limpley Stoke in the Manor House. Unfortunately its records have not survived and so much less is known about it than the boys' Reformatory. Whereas the boys were mainly involved with the farm, the girls' main occupation seems to have been laundry work. They also seem to have stayed for shorter periods at the Reformatory: in 1895, five were admitted, one for three years and four for four years. But the thirteen discharged in that year had served on average just under two years.

The girls' Reformatory seems to have had a much more chequered history than the boys'. By 1870 it had about 70 girls and must already have had some problems for the annual report stated: 'I found the girls in good health and better order than they have been, the influence of the matron (Miss Pike) having gradually made itself more felt among them.' Although the report in 1888 was generally good there was a reference to 'a few exceptional cases and some irregular and wayward tempers and dispositions to control and influence.' Miss Rodman who had been superintendent for a number of years was praised: 'under her judicious and experienced management the results have been most satisfactory.'

Two major incidents occurred in 1873 and 1893 and these were much more serious than anything experienced at the boys' Reformatory. In 1873 the girls refused to do their normal work alleging that they did not have sufficient food. It also transpired that they had taken a dislike to the new laundress and for their disobedience to her their rations had been cut. The girls failed to respond to the persuasion and threats of a local J.P. who had been called to the school so he telegraphed to Bath for police support. A detachment of twenty officers under a Chief Superintendent arrived by train. They managed to arrest eleven of the ringleaders and this was sufficient to restore order. All eleven were tried and were sent to prison for periods ranging from seven days to three months. 'As the prisoners were removed, they were loud in their curses on the head of the manager who was present.'

In 1893 three girls, one 18 year old and two 17 year olds, had been confined to the cells and then to their dormitory for 'refractory conduct'. They managed to break the bars on the window and climb on to the roof where they 'behaved like wild animals' and sang 'hymns, Daisy and low songs'. Again the police had to be called to get them down and to arrest them. All three were charged, two being sent to prison and one returned to the Reformatory.

The Reformatory's closure in 1895 was precipitated by an outbreak of diphtheria. The building has since reverted to a private house.

Sources

The main records of the Wiltshire Reformatory are in the Wiltshire and Swindon
Record Office:

1. Committee minutes:

1743/1 1855-1882
1743/2 1883-1890
1743/3 1891-1925

2. Annual reports and other documents in the Quarter Session records:

A1/515/1 Annual reports 1864-1894 and 1905
A1/515/2 Draft committee reports 1865-1887
A1/515/3 List of donations and subscriptions 1865
3. Conversion of Tascroft 1950-54

2499/301/8 Plans and correspondence.

4. Juvenile offenders

A1/260 Reports of cases involving juvenile offenders in petty sessions 1871-82

5. Diaries

1229/1-6 Diaries of Rev. George Attwood 1913-18

Plans of the major 1901 extension are in the Longleat Archives.

Newspaper reports on the Reformatory and on local cases involving juveniles are
particularly valuable:

Warminster Miscellany 1856-1863
Warminster Herald 1857-1893
Warminster and Westbury Journal 1881-1924